To:

_____

From:

_____

Date:

_____

a Woman's garden of Hope

a Woman's garden of Hope

of Hope

By Dr. Criswell Freeman

ISBN 1-58334-200-1

The quoted ideas expressed in this book (but not scripture verses) are not, in all cases, exact quotations, as some have been edited for clarity and brevity. In all cases, the author has attempted to maintain the speaker's original intent. In some cases, quoted material for this book was obtained from secondary sources, primarily print media. While every effort was made to ensure the accuracy of these sources, the accuracy cannot be guaranteed. For additions, deletions, corrections or clarifications in future editions of this text, please write Brighton Books.

Scripture taken from the HOLY BIBLE, NEW INTERNATIONAL VERSION ©. NIV ©. Copyright © 1973, 1978, 1984, by International Bible Society. Used by permission of Zondervan Publishing House. All rights reserved.

Scripture quotations marked (NLT) are taken from The Holy Bible, New Living Translation, Copyright © 1996. Used by permission of Tyndale House Publishers, Incorporated, Wheaton, Illinois 60189. All rights reserved.

Scripture quotations are taken from the Holman Christian Standard Bible™, Copyright © 1999, 2000, 2001 by Holman Bible Publishers, used by permission.

Scripture taken from the New American Standard Bible®, Copyright © 1960, 1962, 1963, 1968, 1971, 1972, 1973, 1975, 1977, 1995 by The Lockman Foundation. Used by permission.

Printed in the United States of America
Cover Design & Page Layout: Bart Dawson

1 2 3 4 5 6 7 8 9 10 • 03 04 05 06 07 08 09 10

*From The Garden
To Your Heart*

Table of Contents

Introduction

The dictionary defines the word *garden* as "a plot of ground used for the cultivation of flowers, fruits, or vegetables." But those of us who regularly dig our hands into the soil know that a garden is *so much more* than a place for growing plants. It is also a place to renew our spirits as we commune with God and marvel at the beauty of His creation.

A garden can be an oasis of sanity amid the pressures and demands of modern-day living. But many of us lack the opportunity or the time to experience the simple joys of sinking our spades into God's good earth. This little book, while no substitute for the garden, is intended to provide similar comforts and pleasures.

In the garden, we gain perspective. In the garden, we renew our strength. In the garden, we spend quiet moments preparing for the harvest *and* preparing for life. And if we are wise, we also offer thanksgiving and praise to the One who has created us and saved us.

Are you the proud keeper of a tidy little garden? If so, give thanks to God every time you go there. But even if you have no garden to plant, or if your field is currently fallow, take time to consider the words on these pages. And remember that the most important seed you'll ever plant is the seed of God's love—through Christ—that you plant forever in your heart.

A Woman's Garden of Hope

For we are saved by hope . . . .
Romans 8:24 KJV

Hope, like the plants in a garden, must be cultivated with care. If we leave our hopes untended—or if we contaminate them with the twin poisons of discouragement and doubt—the gardens of our souls produce few fruits. But, if we nurture our hopes through a firm faith in God and a realistic faith in ourselves, we bring forth bountiful harvests that bless us, our families, and generations yet unborn.

It is best that we cultivate our hopes each day through quiet meditation, through devotion to God, and through association with encouraging family members and friends. But sometimes, amid the hustle and bustle of life-here-on-earth, we leave our hopes to fend for themselves, and when we do, bad things begin to happen. Like weeds overtaking a flower garden, our worries can quickly overtake our thoughts. The only solution, of course, is to dig in, to pull the weeds, and to reclaim the flowers.

If the garden of your soul has been over-taken by the negativity that is an unfortunate hallmark of the age in which we live, don't be discouraged. Simply turn your thoughts and prayers to the Father and to the Son. Then trust in God's promises. And finally, make the resolution to tend *your* spiritual garden every day that you live. A garden is a lovely place to visit *if* it is tended with care, so cultivate yours carefully, and then reap the bountiful harvest that God has in store for you.

May the God of hope fill you with
all joy and peace as you trust in him,
so that you may overflow with hope
by the power of the Holy Spirit.
Romans 15:13 NIV

*Never yield to gloomy
anticipation. Place your hope
and confidence in God.
He has no record of failure.*

Mrs. Charles E. Cowman

As God's children, we are the recipients
of lavish love—a love that motivates us
to keep trusting even when we have
no idea what God is doing.
Beth Moore

Everything that is done in the world
is done by hope.
Martin Luther

Hope deferred maketh

the heart sick . . . .

Proverbs 13:12 KJV

If my life is surrendered to God,
all is well. Let me not grab it back,
as though it were in peril in His hand
but would be safer in mine!
Elisabeth Elliot

The LORD is good to those whose hope
is in him, to the one who seeks him;
it is good to wait quietly for
the salvation of the LORD.
Lamentations 3:25-26 NIV

Be of good courage, and he shall
strengthen your heart, all ye that
hope in the LORD.
Psalm 31:24 KJV

Now without faith it is impossible
to please God, for the one who draws
near to Him must believe that He exists
and rewards those who seek Him.
Hebrews 11:6 HCSB

Faith in small things has repercussions
that ripple all the way out. In a huge,
dark room a little match can
light up the place.
Joni Eareckson Tada

LORD, sustain me as you promised,
that I may live! Do not let
my hope be crushed.
Psalm 119:116 NLT

But happy are those . . .
whose hope is in
the Lord their God.

Psalm 146:5 NLT

A Prayer from the Garden

Today, Dear Lord, I will live
in hope. If I become
discouraged, I will turn to You.
If I grow weary, I will seek
strength in You. In every aspect
of my life, I will trust You. You
are my Creator and my Savior,
Lord, and I will place my hope
and my faith in You.

Amen

Trusting God

Trust in the LORD with all thine heart;
and lean not unto thine own understanding.
In all thy ways acknowledge him,
and he shall direct thy paths.
Proverbs 3:5-6 KJV

When the seeds of trust are planted in the garden of hope, God brings forth a bountiful harvest. He blesses those who trust in Him, and He offers salvation to those who trust in His Son.

In a letter to first-century Christians, Peter wrote, "And God, in his mighty power, will protect you until you receive this salvation, because you are trusting him" (1 Peter 1:5 NLT). These words have given assurance and comfort to believers of every generation.

On occasion, you will confront circumstances that trouble you to the very core of your soul. When you are afraid, trust in God. When you are worried, turn your concerns over to Him. When you are anxious, be still and listen for the quiet assurance of God's promises. And then, place your life in God's hands. He will never fail you. So trust Him today and forever.

*The Lord is my rock,
and my fortress, and my deliverer;
my God, my strength,
in whom I will trust . . . .*

Psalm 18:2 KJV

*Never be afraid to trust
an unknown future
to a known God.*

Corrie ten Boom

It is one thing to love the ways of
the Lord when all is well and quite
another thing to cling to them during
discouragement or difficulty.
C. H. Spurgeon

Once we recognize our need for Jesus,
then the building of our faith begins.
It is a daily, moment-by-moment life
of absolute dependence upon Him
for everything.
Catherine Marshall

When the train goes through a tunnel and the world becomes dark, do you jump out? Of course not. You sit still and trust the engineer to get you through.
Corrie ten Boom

Brother, is your faith looking upward today? Trust in the promise of the Savior. Sister, is the light shining bright on your way?
Trust in the promise of thy Lord.
Fanny Crosby

What time I am afraid,
I will trust in thee.
Psalm 56:3 KJV

I do beg of you to recognize the extreme simplicity of faith; it is nothing more nor less than just believing God when He says He either has done something for us, or will do it; and then trusting Him to do it. It is so simple that it is hard to explain.
Hannah Whitall Smith

What is courage? It is the ability to be strong in trust, in conviction, in obedience. To be courageous is to step out in faith— to trust and obey, no matter what.
Kay Arthur

Trust in yourself and you are doomed to disappointment; trust in money and you may have it taken from you, but trust in God, and you are never to be confounded in time or eternity.
D. L. Moody

A Prayer from the Garden

Today, Lord, I will trust You and seek Your will for my life. You have a plan for me, Dear Lord. Let me discover it and live it, knowing that when I trust in You, I am eternally blessed. *Amen*

God's Grace

*For it is by grace you have been saved,
through faith—and this not from yourselves,
it is the gift of God—not by works, so that
no one can boast.*
Ephesians 2:8-9 NIV

All of us have more blessings than we can count. We have received countless gifts from God, but none can compare with the treasure that is the gift of salvation. When we accept Christ into our hearts, we are saved by God's grace. The familiar words of Ephesians 2:8 make God's promise perfectly clear: we are saved not by our actions but by God's mercy. We are saved not because of our good deeds but because of our faith in Christ.

Grace is the ultimate gift, and we owe God the ultimate in thanksgiving. Let us praise the Creator for His priceless gift, and let us share the good news with all who cross our paths. We return our Creator's love by accepting His grace and by sharing His message and His love. When we do, we are blessed here on earth and throughout all eternity.

Grace to you and peace from God
our Father and the Lord Jesus Christ.
Philippians 1:2 NASB

Grace calls you to get up, throw off
your blanket of helplessness, and
to move on through life in faith.
Kay Arthur

If you have a true faith that Christ is
your Savior, then at once you have
a gracious God, for faith leads you in
and opens up God's heart and will,
that you should see pure grace
and overflowing love.
Martin Luther

God is the giver, and we are the receivers. And His richest gifts are bestowed not upon those who do the greatest things, but upon those who accept His abundance and His grace.

Hannah Whitall Smith

True have His promises been; not one has
failed. I want none beside Him. In life He
is my life, and in death He shall be the
death of death; in poverty, Christ is my
riches; in sickness, He makes my bed; in
darkness, He is my star, and in brightness,
He is my sun. Jesus is to me all grace and
no wrath, all truth and no falsehood; and
of truth and grace He is full, infinitely full.
C. H. Spurgeon

How beautiful it is to learn that grace
isn't fragile, and that in the family of God
we can fail and not be a failure.
Gloria Gaither

Christ is no Moses, no exactor, no giver
of laws, but a giver of grace, a Savior;
He is infinite mercy and goodness,
freely and bountifully given to us.
Martin Luther

Yes, God's grace is always sufficient,
and His arms are always open to give it.
But, will our arms be open to receive it?
Beth Moore

We will never cease to need our Father—
His wisdom, direction, help, and support.
We will never outgrow Him.
We will always need His grace.
Kay Arthur

*Therefore let us approach
the throne of grace with boldness,
so that we may receive mercy
and find grace to help us
at the proper time.*

Hebrews 4:16 HCSB

A Prayer from the Garden

Lord, You have saved me
by Your grace. Keep me mindful that Your grace is a gift that
I can accept but cannot earn.
I praise You for that priceless
gift, today and forever. Let me
share the good news of
Your grace with a world
that desperately needs
Your healing touch.

Amen

Hope for the Future

*So don't worry, saying, "What will we eat?" or
"What will we drink?" or "What will we wear?"
For the Gentiles eagerly seek all these things, and
your heavenly Father knows that you need them.
But seek first the kingdom of God and His
righteousness, and all these things will be provided
for you. Therefore don't worry about tomorrow,
because tomorrow will worry about itself.
ach day has enough trouble of its own.*
Matthew 6:31-34 HCSB

Every garden is a leap of faith. Every garden is a statement of trust in the future. Every garden is a declaration of hope. We sow our seeds in the springtime, hoping to reap a harvest that is eagerly anticipated but, as of yet, unseen. And so it is with life. Each day, as we tend to the necessities of life, we plant seeds for the future. When we plant wisely and trust God completely, the harvest is bountiful.

When we trust God, we must trust Him without reservation. We must steel ourselves against the inevitable disappointments of the day, secure in the knowledge that our Heavenly Father has a plan for the future that we cannot see.

Can you place your future into the hands of a loving and all-knowing God? Can you live amid the uncertainties of today, knowing that God has dominion over all your tomorrows? If you can, you are wise and you are blessed. When you trust God with everything you are and everything you have, He will give you strength and life, not just for today but for all eternity.

But Jesus turned him about,
and when he saw her, he said,
Daughter, be of good comfort;
thy faith hath made thee whole.
And the woman was made
whole from that hour.

Matthew 9:22 KJV

Hope must be in the future tense.
Faith, to be faith, must always
be in the present tense.

Catherine Marshall

Love is the seed of all hope.
It is the enticement to trust, to risk,
to try, and to go on.
Gloria Gaither

Everything that is done in
the world is done by hope.
Martin Luther

Our hope in Christ for the future is
the mainstream of our joy.
C. H. Spurgeon

Oh, the tranquil joy of that dear retreat,
Where the Savior bids thee rest,
With steadfast hope, and a trusting faith,
In His love secure and blest.
Fanny Crosby

Many sorrows come to the wicked,
but unfailing love surrounds
those who trust the LORD.
Psalm 32:10 NLT

Easter comes each year to remind us of a truth that is eternal and universal. The empty tomb of Easter morning says to you and me, "Of course you'll encounter trouble. But behold a God of power who can take any evil and turn it into a door of hope."

Catherine Marshall

A Prayer from the Garden

Dear Lord, I come to You today
with hope in my heart and
praise on my lips. I place
my trust in You, Dear God,
knowing that with You as my
Protector, I have nothing to
fear. I thank You, Father, for
Your grace, for Your Love, and
for Your Son. Let me follow in
Christ's footsteps today and
every day that I live. And then,
when my work here is done, let
me live with You forever.

Amen

Hope for Our Families

Choose for yourselves this day whom you will serve . . . as for me and my household, we will serve the LORD.
Joshua 24:15 NIV

*W*ho taught you the finer points of gardening? If you learned from your parents or grandparents, you are lucky indeed. If you have grown up as a member of a close-knit, supportive family, offer a word of thanks to God.

Your family is a priceless gift from the Creator. Treasure it, protect it, and dedicate it to Him. When you place God at the center of your family, He will bless you and yours in ways that you could have scarcely imagined.

The world is filled with dangers and temptations. But, when you place your trust in God, you can entertain great hopes for yourself *and* for your loved ones. May you trust Him always and obey His commandments. When you do, you are secure in His love today and forever.

These should learn first of all to put their religion into practice by caring for their own family . . .

1 Timothy 5:4 NIV

It is a reverent thing to see an ancient
castle or building not in decay, or to see
a fair timber tree sound and perfect.
How much more beautiful it is to behold
an ancient and noble family that has stood
against the waves and weathers of time.
Francis Bacon

A home is a place where we find direction.
Gigi Graham Tchividjian

A family is a place where principles
are hammered and honed on
the anvil of everyday living.
Charles Swindoll

Love must be without hypocrisy. Detest
evil; cling to what is good. Show family
affection to one another with brotherly
love. Outdo one another
in showing honor.
Romans 12:9-10 HCSB

The secret of a happy home life is that
the members of the family learn
to give and receive love.
Billy Graham

I give you a new commandment: that you
love one another. Just as I have loved you,
you should also love one another. By this
all people will know that you are
My disciples, if you have love
for one another.
John 13:34-35 HCSB

A Prayer from the Garden

Dear Lord, I am part of Your family, and I praise You for Your gifts and for Your love. You have also blessed me with my earthly family, and I pray for them, that they might be protected and blessed by You. Let me show love and acceptance for my family, Lord, so that through me, they might come to know and to love You.

Amen

When Our

Hearts

Are Heavy

*Blessed are the poor in spirit: for theirs is
the kingdom of heaven. Blessed are they
that mourn: for they shall be comforted.
Matthew 5:3-4 KJV*

Sometimes, we retreat to the garden with heavy hearts. Grief visits all of us who live long and love deeply. When we lose a loved one, or when we experience any other profound loss, darkness overwhelms us for a while, and it seems as if we cannot summon the strength to face another day—but, with God's help, we can.

Thankfully, God promises that He is "close to the brokenhearted" (Psalm 34:18 NIV). In times of intense sadness, we must turn to Him, and we must encourage our friends and family members to do likewise. When we do, our Father comforts us and, in time, He heals us.

*Cast your burden upon
the Lord and He will sustain
you: He will never allow
the righteous to be shaken.*

Psalm 55:22 NASB

We look at our burdens and heavy loads,
and we shrink from them. But, if we lift
them and bind them about our hearts,
they become wings, and on them we can
rise and soar toward God.

Mrs. Charles E. Cowman

God of our life, there are days when the
burdens we carry chafe our shoulders and
weigh us down; when the road seems
dreary and endless, the skies gray and
threatening; when our lives have no music
in them, and our hearts are lonely, and
our souls have lost their courage. Flood the
path with light, run our eyes to where the
skies are full of promise; tune our hearts to
brave music; give us the sense
of comradeship with heroes and saints of
every age; and so quicken our spirits that
we may be able to encourage the souls of
all who journey with us on the road of life,
to Your honor and glory.

St. Augustine

Like Paul, we may bear thorns so that we
can discover God's perfect sufficiency.
Beth Moore

As we wait on God, He helps us use
the winds of adversity to soar above our
problems. As the Bible says, "Those who
wait on the LORD . . . shall mount up
with wings like eagles."
Billy Graham

God allows us to experience the low points
of life in order to teach us lessons that
we could learn in no other way.
C. S. Lewis

God walks with us. He scoops us up in
His arms or simply sits with us in silent
strength until we cannot avoid
the awesome recognition that yes,
even now, He is here.
Gloria Gaither

Often God shuts a door in our face so
that He can open the door through
which He wants us to go.
Catherine Marshall

It is better to take refuge in
the LORD than to trust in man.
Psalm 118:8 NIV

When my heart is overwhelmed: lead me
to the rock that is higher than I.
Psalm 61:2 KJV

God's curriculum for all who sincerely
want to know Him and do His will always
includes lessons we wish we could skip.
With an intimate understanding of our
deepest needs and individual capacities,
He chooses our curriculum.
Elisabeth Elliot

But I will call on God, and the LORD
will rescue me. Morning, noon, and
night I plead aloud in my distress, and
the LORD hears my voice.
Psalm 55:16-17 NLT

A Prayer from the Garden

Heavenly Father, Your Word
promises that You will not give
us more than we can bear; You
have promised to lift us out of
our grief and despair. Today,
Lord, I pray for those who
mourn, and I thank You for
sustaining all of us in our days
of sorrow. May we trust You
always and praise You forever.

Amen

God's Presence

Be still, and know that I am God.
Psalm 46:10 KJV

In the early morning, as the sun's first rays peek over the horizon, we sense the presence of God. But as the day wears on and the demands of everyday life bear down upon us, we may become so wrapped up in earthy concerns that we forget to praise the Creator.

God is everywhere we have ever been and everywhere we will ever be. He is in the quietest corner of the garden or on the loudest corner of the city street. When we turn to Him often, we are blessed by His presence. But, if we ignore God's presence or—worse yet—rebel against it altogether, the world in which we live soon becomes a spiritual wasteland.

Are you tired, discouraged or fearful? Be comforted because God is with you. Are you confused? Listen to the quiet voice of your Heavenly Father. Are you bitter? Talk with God and seek His guidance. Are you celebrating a great victory? Thank God and praise Him. He is the Giver of all things good. In whatever condition you find yourself, wherever you are, whether you are happy or sad, victorious or vanquished, troubled or triumphant, celebrate God's presence. And be comforted. God is not just near. He is here.

*Draw close to God,
and God will draw close to you.*

James 4:8 NLT

If your heart has grown cold,
it is because you have moved away from
the fire of His presence.
Beth Moore

If you want to hear God's voice clearly
and you are uncertain, then remain in
His presence until He changes that
uncertainty. Often, much can happen
during this waiting for the Lord.
Sometimes, he changes pride into
humility, doubt into faith and peace.
Corrie ten Boom

Our souls were made to live in an upper
atmosphere, and we stifle and choke if
we live on any lower level. Our eyes were
made to look off from these heavenly
heights, and our vision is distorted
by any lower gazing.
Hannah Whitall Smith

It is not possible that mortal men should
be thoroughly conscious of the divine
presence without being filled with awe.
C. H. Spurgeon

The secret is Christ in me, not me in
a different set of circumstances.
Elisabeth Elliot

A Prayer from the Garden

Heavenly Father, help me to feel Your presence in every situation and every circumstance. You are with me, Lord, in times of celebration and in times of sorrow. You are with me when I am strong and when I am weak. You never leave my side even when it seems to me that You are far away. Today and every day, God, let me feel You and acknowledge Your presence so that others, too, might know You through me.

Amen

Hope for Spiritual Growth

But grow in the grace and knowledge of our Lord and Savior Jesus Christ. To Him be the glory, both now and to the day of eternity.
2 Peter 3:18 NASB

Plants of every sort respond to nourishment, and so it is with human hearts. When we begin each day with heads bowed and hearts lifted, we remind ourselves of God's love, His protection, and His commandments. If we are wise, we align our priorities for the coming day with the teachings and commandments that God has given us through His Holy Word. And because we nourish our souls, we continue to grow "in the grace and knowledge of our Lord."

The journey toward spiritual maturity lasts a lifetime. As Christians, we can and should continue to grow in our devotion to the Savior as long as we live. When we cease to grow, either emotionally or spiritually, we do ourselves a profound disservice. But, if we study God's Word, if we obey His commandments, and if we live in the center of His will, we will not be "stagnant" believers; we will, instead, be growing Christians . . . and that's exactly what God intends for us to become.

*Therefore let us leave
the elementary teachings about
Christ and go on to maturity . . . .*

❦

Hebrews 6:1 NIV

Know the love of Christ which surpasses
knowledge, that you may be filled up
to all the fullness of God.
Ephesians 3:19 NASB

The maturity of a Christian experience
cannot be reached in a moment, but is
the result of the work of God's Holy Spirit,
who, by His energizing and transforming
power, causes us to grow up into
Christ in all things.
Hannah Whitall Smith

We are in a continual battle with
the spiritual forces of evil, but we will
triumph when we yield to God's
leading and call on His
powerful presence in prayer.
Shirley Dobson

Take my yoke upon you
and learn from me . . . .
Matthew 11:29 NIV

No matter how efficient, smart, or
independent we happen to think ourselves
to be, sooner or later we run into a brick
wall that our intelligence or experience
cannot handle for us. We can fake it, avoid
it, or blunder through it. But, a better
solution would be to find someone who
has walked that way before and has
gained wisdom from experience.
Gloria Gaither

Walking in faith brings you to the Word of
God. There you will be healed, cleansed,
fed, nurtured, equipped, and matured.
Kay Arthur

Recently I've been learning that life comes down to this: God is in everything. Regardless of what difficulties I am experiencing at the moment, or what things aren't as I would like them to be, I look at the circumstances and say, "Lord, what are you trying to teach me?"
Catherine Marshall

Our vision is so limited we can hardly imagine a love that does not show itself in protection from suffering. The love of God did not protect His own Son. He will not necessarily protect us—not from anything it takes to make us like His Son. A lot of hammering and chiseling and purifying by fire will have to go into the process.
Elisabeth Elliot

I'm not what I want to be.
I'm not what I'm going to be.
But, thank God, I'm not what I was!
Gloria Gaither

Grow, dear friends, but grow,
I beseech you, in God's way,
which is the only true way.

Hannah Whitall Smith

A Prayer from the Garden

Thank You, Lord, that I am not
yet what I am to become.
The Holy Scripture tells me
that You are at work in my life,
continuing to help me grow
and to mature in the faith.
Show me Your wisdom, Father,
and let me live according to
Your Word and Your will.

Amen

Hope for Troubled Times

*Be joyful in hope, patient in affliction,
faithful in prayer.*
Romans 12:12 NIV

Sometimes, our harvests are bountiful; sometimes they are not. But during life's darker days, there is a source of strength upon which we, as Christians, must depend.

In times of trouble, God stands ready to protect us. Our responsibility, of course, is to ask Him for protection. When we do, He hears our prayers, and He answers those prayers in His own way and in His own time.

Are you worried or confused? Does your future seem foreboding? Are you anxious about your finances, your health, or your relationships? If so, you must turn your concerns over to a power far greater than your own.

Whether your harvest is bountiful or not, lift your prayers to the Father whose love for you is infinite and eternal. He will never fail you.

May the God of hope fill
you with all joy and peace as
you trust in him, so that you may
overflow with hope by
the power of the Holy Spirit.

Romans 15:13 NIV

Put your hand into the hand of God. He gives the calmness and serenity of heart and soul.

Mrs. Charles E. Cowman

Make the least of all that goes and
the most of all that comes. Don't regret
what is past. Cherish what you have.
Look forward to all that is to come. And
most important of all, rely moment
by moment on Jesus Christ.
Gigi Graham Tchividjian

Often, in the midst of great problems,
we stop short of the real blessing God has
for us, which is a fresh vision of who He is.
Anne Graham Lotz

Measure the size of the obstacles
against the size of God.
Beth Moore

God makes the sunshine every day,
even though it is sometimes hidden
behind the clouds.
Corrie ten Boom

If your every human plan and calculation
has miscarried, if, one by one, human
props have been knocked out . . . take
heart. God is trying to get a message
through to you, and the message is:
"Stop depending on inadequate human
resources. Let me handle the matter."
Catherine Marshall

Often the trials we mourn are really
gateways into the good things
we long for.
Hannah Whitall Smith

If God sends us on stony paths,
He provides strong shoes.
Corrie ten Boom

It may be that the day of judgment will
dawn tomorrow; in that case, we shall
gladly stop working for a better tomorrow.
But not before.
Dietrich Bonhoeffer

We ought to give thanks for all fortune:
if it is good, because it is good, if bad,
because it works in us patience, humility,
and the contempt of this world, along with
the hope of our eternal country.
C. S. Lewis

This hard place in which you perhaps find
yourself is the very place in which God
is giving you opportunity to look only to
Him, to spend time in prayer, and to learn
long-suffering, gentleness, meekness—in
short, to learn the depths of the love that
Christ Himself has poured out on all of us.
Elisabeth Elliot

Weave the unveiling fabric of God's Word
through your heart and mind. It will hold
strong, even if the rest of life unravels.
Gigi Graham Tchividjian

The righteous face many troubles,
but the LORD rescues them from
each and every one.
Psalm 34:19 NLT

The disappointment has come, not because
God desires to hurt you or make you mis-
erable or to demoralize you, or ruin your
life, or keep you from ever
knowing happiness. He wants you to be
perfect and complete in every aspect,
lacking nothing. It's not the easy times
that make you more like Jesus,
but the hard times.
Kay Arthur

We also rejoice in our sufferings,
because we know that suffering produces
perseverance; perseverance, character;
and character, hope.
Romans 5:3-4 NIV

A Prayer from the Garden

Dear Lord, You are my strength. When I am troubled, You comfort me. When I am discouraged, You lift me up. Whatever my circumstances, Lord, let me trust Your plan for my life. And, when my family and friends are troubled, let me remind them of Your love, Your wisdom, and Your grace.

Amen

And the Greatest
of These . . .

But now abide faith, hope, love, these three;
but the greatest of these is love.
1 Corinthians 13:13 NASB

hrist's words left no room for interpretation: "'Love the Lord your God with all your heart and with all your soul and with all your mind.' This is the first and greatest commandment. And the second is like it: 'Love your neighbor as yourself.' All the Law and the Prophets hang on these two commandments" (Matthew 22:37-40 NIV). But sometimes, despite our best intentions, we fall short. When we become embittered with ourselves, with our neighbors, or most especially with God, we disobey the One who gave His life for us.

If we are to please God, we must cleanse ourselves of the negative feelings that separate us from others and from Him. In 1 Corinthians 13, we are told that love is the foundation upon which all our relationships are to be built: our relationships with others *and* our relationship with our Maker. May we fill our hearts with love; may we never yield to bitterness. And may we praise the Son of God who, in His infinite wisdom, made love His greatest commandment.

Love is patient, love is kind and
is not jealous; love does not brag
and is not arrogant, does not act
unbecomingly; it does not seek its
own, is not provoked, does not take
into account a wrong suffered, does
not rejoice in unrighteousness, but
rejoices with the truth; bears all
things, believes all things, hopes
all things, endures all things.

1 Corinthians 13:4-7 NASB

It is when we come to the Lord in our
nothingness, our powerlessness and our
helplessness that He then enables us
to love in a way which, without Him,
would be absolutely impossible.
Elisabeth Elliot

Line by line, moment by moment,
special times are etched into our memories
in the permanent ink of everlasting love
in our relationships.
Gloria Gaither

He who is filled with love is filled
with God Himself.
St. Augustine

See that ye love one another
with a pure heart fervently.
1 Peter 1:22 KJV

Inasmuch as love grows in you,
so beauty grows. For love is
the beauty of the soul.
St. Augustine

In true religion, to love God and
to know God are synonymous terms.
C. H. Spurgeon

A Prayer from the Garden

Lord, You have given me
love that is beyond human
understanding, and I am Your
loving servant. May the love
that I feel for You be reflected
in the compassion that I show
toward others. Give me Your
eyes to see others as You see
them, Lord, and let me be
generous and kind to those
who cross my path
this day and every day.

Amen

A Prayer for God's Peace

And the peace of God, which surpasses all comprehension, will guard your hearts and your minds in Christ Jesus. Philippians 4:7 NASB

We are drawn to our gardens, in part, because they are havens of peace. Amid the hustle and bustle of everyday life, the garden remains a place of quiet comfort. But no place on earth, no matter how peaceful, can offer us lasting contentment *unless* we first discover peace in God.

The peace that God offers is beyond human understanding. It is a peace that heals us, comforts us, protects us, and transforms us.

By accepting God's peace, we "guard our hearts and minds in Christ Jesus," *and* we enjoy the spiritual abundance that He has promised to those who love Him and obey His commandments. May we accept God's peace, and may we share it freely today, tomorrow, and forever.

These things I have spoken unto
you, that in me ye might have
peace. In the world ye shall have
tribulation: but be of good cheer;
I have overcome the world.

John 16:33 KJV

To know God as He really is—in His
essential nature and character—is to arrive
at a citadel of peace that circumstances
may storm, but can never capture.
Catherine Marshall

Look around you and you'll be dis-
tressed; look within yourself and you'll be
depressed; look at Jesus,
and you'll be at rest!
Corrie ten Boom

He Himself is our peace.
Ephesians 2:14 NASB

Those who are God's without reserve are, in every sense, content.

Hannah Whitall Smith

When something robs you of your peace
of mind, ask yourself if it is worth
the energy you are expending on it.
If not, then put it out of your mind in an
act of discipline. Every time the thought
of "it" returns, refuse it.
Kay Arthur

May the God of hope fill you with all
joy and peace as you trust in him, so that
you may overflow with hope by
the power of the Holy Spirit.
Romans 15:13 NIV

And let the peace of God rule in
your hearts . . . and be ye thankful.
Colossians 3:15 KJV

*Peace I leave with you,
my peace I give unto you:
not as the world giveth, give
I unto you. Let not your heart
be troubled, neither let it be afraid.*

John 14:27 KJV

A Prayer from the Garden

Dear Lord, the peace that
the world offers is fleeting,
but You offer a peace that is
perfect and eternal. Let me turn
the cares and burdens of my life
over to You, Father, and let me
feel the spiritual abundance
that You offer through
the person of Your Son,
the Prince of Peace.

Amen

Expecting
Miracles

For with God nothing shall be impossible.
Luke 1:37 KJV

When we pause to consider the glory of God's creation, we marvel at the miracle of nature. The smallest seedlings and grandest stars are all part of God's infinite universe, and He made them all. The same God who brought light out of darkness can work miracles in your own life *if* you have faith.

Jesus said, "I tell you the truth, if you have faith as small as a mustard seed, you can say to this mountain, 'Move from here to there' and it will move. Nothing will be impossible for you." We must trust Christ's promise.

Sometimes, because we are imperfect human beings with limited understanding and limited faith, we place limitations on God. But, God's power has no limitations. God will work miracles in our lives if we trust Him with everything we have and everything we are. When we do, we will experience the miraculous results of His endless love and His awesome power.

Jesus said to them,
"I have shown you many great
miracles from the Father."

John 10:32 NIV

I could go through this day oblivious to
the miracles all around me,
or I could tune in and enjoy.
Gloria Gaither

Our helplessness can be a healthy sign.
This is always a good place to begin a task
that seems completely impossible.
Catherine Marshall

Blessed are they that have not seen,
and yet have believed.
John 20:29 KJV

We have a God who delights
in impossibilities.
Andrew Murray

Jesus said unto him, If thou canst believe,
all things are possible to him
that believeth.
Mark 9:23 KJV

Then Jesus answered,
"Woman, you have great faith!
Your request is granted."
And her daughter was healed
from that very hour.

Matthew 15:28 NIV

Only God can move mountains,
but faith and prayer
can move God.

E. M. Bounds

A Prayer from the Garden

Dear God, nothing is impossible for You. Your infinite power is beyond human understanding—keep me always mindful of Your strength. When I lose hope, give me faith; when others lose hope, let me tell them of Your glory and Your works. Today, Lord, let me expect the miraculous, and let me trust in You.

Amen

Praying for an Obedient Heart

For whosoever shall do the will of God,
the same is my brother, and my sister, and mother.
Mark 3:35 KJV

God's laws are eternal and unchanging: obedience leads to abundance and joy; disobedience leads to disaster. God has given us a guidebook for righteous living called the Holy Bible. If we trust God's Word and live by it, we are blessed. But, if we choose to ignore God's commandments, the results are as predictable as they are tragic.

Life is a series of decisions and choices. Each day, we make countless decisions that can bring us closer to God . . . or not. When we live according to God's commandments, we earn for ourselves the abundance and peace that He intends for our lives.

Do you seek God's peace and His blessings? Then obey Him. When you're faced with a difficult choice or a powerful temptation, seek God's counsel and trust the counsel He gives. Invite God into your heart and live according to His commandments. When you do, you will be blessed today and tomorrow and forever.

Whoever has my commands
and obeys them, he is the one who
loves me. He who loves me will
be loved by my Father, and
I too will love him
and show myself to him.

John 14:21 NIV

God does not want the forced obedience
of slaves. Instead, He covets the voluntary
love and obedience of children who love
Him for Himself.
Catherine Marshall

Our obedience does not make God
any bigger or better than He already is.
Anything God commands of us is so that
our joy may be full—the joy of seeing His
glory revealed to us and in us!
Beth Moore

Rejoicing is a matter of obedience to
God—an obedience that will start you on
the road to peace and contentment.
Kay Arthur

Now if we have died with Christ, we
believe that we shall also live with Him.
Romans 6:8 HCSB

Faith is obedience at home and
looking to the Master; obedience is faith
going out to do His will.
Andrew Murray

It is the LORD your God you must follow,
and him you must revere. Keep his
commands and obey him; serve him
and hold fast to him.
Deuteronomy 13:4 NIV

A Prayer from the Garden

Lord, when I turn my thoughts away from You and Your Word, I suffer. But when I obey Your commandments, when I place my faith in You, I am secure. Let me live according to Your commandments. Direct my path far from the temptations and distractions of this world. And, let me discover Your will and follow it, Dear Lord, this day and always.

Amen

A Prayer
for Renewal

Come to me, all you who are weary and burdened,
and I will give you rest. Take my yoke upon you
and learn from me, for I am gentle and humble in
heart, and you will find rest for your souls.
For my yoke is easy and my burden is light.
Matthew 11:28-30 NIV

In the garden, we witness the cycle of the harvest: we sow, we reap, and then, as our fields lie fallow, we take time to rest. God intends that His children reap bountiful harvests, and when our spiritual fields are barren, He offers us renewal and strength.

Are you tired or troubled? Turn your heart toward God in prayer. Are you weak or worried? Take the time—or, more accurately, make the time—to delve deeply into God's Holy Word. Are you spiritually depleted? Call upon fellow believers to support you, and call upon Christ to renew your spirit and your life. When you do, you'll discover that the Creator of the universe stands always ready and always able to create a new sense of wonderment and joy in you.

Create in me a clean heart,
O God; and renew
a right spirit within me.

Psalm 51:10 KJV

The amazing thing about Jesus is that He doesn't just patch up our lives; He gives us a brand new sheet, a clean slate to start over, all new.

Gloria Gaither

Therefore if anyone is in Christ, he is
a new creature; the old things passed away;
behold, new things have come.
2 Corinthians 5:17 HCSB

The same voice that brought Lazarus out
of the tomb raised us to newness of life.
C. H. Spurgeon

Repentance removes old sins and wrong
attitudes, and it opens the way for
the Holy Spirit to restore
our spiritual health.
Shirley Dobson

Sometimes, we need
a housecleaning of the heart.
Catherine Marshall

And Jesus called a little child unto him,
and set him in the midst of them, and said,
Verily I say unto you, Except ye be
converted, and become as little
children, ye shall not enter into
the kingdom of heaven.
Matthew 18:2-3 KJV

*And He who sits on
the throne said, "Behold,
I am making all things new."*

Revelation 21:5 NASB

A Prayer from the Garden

Lord, I am an imperfect
woman. Because my faith
is limited, I may become
overwhelmed by the demands
of the day. When I feel tired or
discouraged, renew my strength.
When I am worried, let me turn
my thoughts and my prayers
to You. Let me trust Your
promises, Dear Lord, and
let me accept Your unending
love, now and forever.

Amen

Faith in God's Blessings

For thou, LORD, wilt bless the righteous . . . .
Psalm 5:12 KJV

In the garden, we should pause to consider God's blessings. God's gifts are, of course, too numerous to count, but as believers, we should attempt to count them nonetheless.

Our blessings include life, family, nature, friends, talents, and possessions, for starters. And our greatest gift—a treasure that is ours for the asking—is God's gift of salvation through Christ Jesus.

Today, let us thank our Creator for His blessings. And let us demonstrate our gratitude to the Giver of all things good by using His gifts *and* by sharing them.

*Now faith is the reality
of what is hoped for,
the proof of what is not seen.*

Hebrews 11:1 HCSB

*God has promised that if we
harvest well with the tools
of thanksgiving, there will
be seeds for planting in the spring.*

Gloria Gaither

Jesus intended for us to be overwhelmed
by the blessings of regular days. He said it
was the reason He had come: "I am come
that they might have life, and that they
might have it more abundantly."
Gloria Gaither

Oh! what a Savior, gracious to all,
Oh! how His blessings round us fall,
Gently to comfort, kindly to cheer,
Sleeping or waking, God is near.
Fanny Crosby

Do we not continually pass by blessings
innumerable without notice, and instead
fix our eyes on what we feel to be our trials
and our losses, and think and talk about
these until our whole horizon is filled with
them, and we almost begin to think we
have no blessings at all?
Hannah Whitall Smith

Bless the LORD, O my soul,
and forget not all his benefits.
Psalm 103:2 KJV

God is more anxious to bestow His blessings on us than we are to receive them.

St. Augustine

A Prayer from the Garden

Today, Lord, let me count my blessings with thanksgiving in my heart. You have cared for me, Lord, and I will give You the glory and the praise. Let me accept Your blessings and Your gifts, and let me share them with others, just as You first shared them with me.

Amen

The Assurance
of Salvation

For God so loved the world, that he gave
his only begotten Son, that whosoever believeth
in him should not perish, but have everlasting life.
John 3:16 KJV

Christ sacrificed His life on the cross so that we might have eternal life. This gift, freely given by God's only begotten Son, is the priceless possession of everyone who accepts Him as Lord and Savior. God is waiting patiently for each of us to accept the gift of eternal life. Let us claim Christ's gift today.

It is by God's grace that we have been saved, through faith. We are saved not because of our good deeds but because of our faith in Christ. May we, who have been given so much, praise our Savior for the gift of salvation, and may we share the joyous news of our Master's love and His grace.

Then spake Jesus again unto them, saying, I am the light of the world: he that followeth me shall not walk in darkness, but shall have the light of life.

John 8:12 KJV

I now know the power of the risen Lord! He lives! The dawn of Easter has broken in my own soul! My night is gone!

Mrs. Charles E. Cowman

In the depths of our sin, Christ died for us.
He did not wait for persons to get as
close as possible through obedience to
the law and righteous living.
Beth Moore

I have been all over the world, and
I have never met anyone who regretted
giving his or her life to Christ.
Billy Graham

The redemption, accomplished for us
by our Lord Jesus Christ on the cross at
Calvary, is redemption from the power of
sin as well as from its guilt. Christ is able
to save all who come unto God by Him.
Hannah Whitall Smith

He saved us, not on the basis of deeds
which we have done in righteousness, but
according to His mercy, by the washing
of regeneration and renewing by the Holy
Spirit, whom He poured out upon us richly
through Jesus Christ our Savior . . . .
Titus 3:5-6 NASB

Though the details may differ from story
to story, we are all sinners—saved only
by the wonderful grace of God.
Gloria Gaither

The truth of Christ brings assurance and
so removes the former problem
of fear and uncertainty.
A. W. Tozer

He alone is my rock and my salvation;
he is my fortress, I will never be shaken.
Psalm 62:2 NIV

For whoever wishes to save his life will lose
it; but whoever loses his life for My sake
will find it. For what will it profit a man
if he gains the whole world and forfeits
his soul? Or what will a man give in
exchange for his soul?
Matthew 16:25-26 HCSB

But God demonstrates his own love for
us in this: While we were still sinners,
Christ died for us.
Romans 5:8 NIV

A Prayer from the Garden

My salvation is in You, O
Lord. My soul finds rest in You
through Your Son, Jesus Christ.
The gift of salvation brings
meaning to my life here on
earth just as surely as it
prepares me for eternal life
with You in heaven. Let me
praise You and give thanks for
Your glorious gift . . .
and let me share it to all
who cross my path.

Amen

Trusting God's Will

*Trust in the LORD with all thine heart; and
lean not unto thine own understanding. In all thy ways
acknowledge him, and he shall direct thy paths.
Proverbs 3:5-6 KJV*

When Jesus went to the Mount of Olives, He poured out His heart to God. Jesus knew of the agony that He was destined to endure, but He also knew that God's will must be done. We, like our Savior, face trials that bring fear and trembling to the very depths of our souls, but like Christ, we too must ultimately seek God's will, not our own.

God makes His plans clear to those who genuinely and humbly seek His will. As this day unfolds, let us seek God's will and obey His Word. When we entrust our lives to Him completely and without reservation, He gives us the strength to meet any challenge, the courage to face any trial, and the wisdom to live in His righteousness and in His peace.

*Commit everything you do to
the Lord. Trust him,
and he will help you.*

Psalm 37:5 NLT

No matter how fervent our desires and
requests, the Lord does not always respond
the way we would choose. Sometimes His
answers to our petitions
are the very opposite of what we've
sought, yet He always has
our best interests in mind.
Shirley Dobson

Absolute submission is not enough;
we should go on to joyful acquiescence
to the will of God.
C. H. Spurgeon

I trust in You, O LORD, I say,
"You are my God." My times
are in Your hand.
Psalm 31:14-15 NASB

Jesus told us that only in God's will
would we have real freedom.
Catherine Marshall

If God, like a father, denies us what we
want now, it is in order to give us some
far better thing later on. The will of God,
we can rest assured, is invariably
a better thing.
Elisabeth Elliot

To yield to God means to belong to God,
and to belong to God means to have
all His infinite power. To belong
to God means to have all.
Hannah Whitall Smith

Part of waiting upon the Lord is telling
God that you want only what He wants—
whatever it is.
Kay Arthur

If in the integrity of my heart I speak
the words, *Thy will be done*, I must be
willing, if the answer requires it, that *my*
will be undone. It is a prayer of
commitment and relinquishment.
Elisabeth Elliot

If you are struggling to make some difficult
decisions right now that aren't specifically
addressed in the Bible, don't make
a choice based on what's right for
someone else. You are the Lord's, and
He will make sure you do what's right.
Lisa Whelchel

Yielding to the will of God is simply letting
His Holy Spirit have His way in our lives.
Shirley Dobson

Only God's chosen task for you will
ultimately satisfy. Do not wait until it is
too late to realize the privilege of serving
Him in His chosen position for you.
Beth Moore

And this world is fading away, along
with everything it craves. But if you do
the will of God, you will live forever.
1 John 2:17 NLT

A Prayer from the Garden

Lord, let Your will be my will.
When I am confused, give me
maturity and wisdom. When I
am worried, give me courage
and strength. Let me be Your
faithful servant, Father, always
seeking Your guidance
and Your will for my life.

Amen

With Hope and
Thanksgiving

*Make a joyful noise unto the LORD all ye lands.
Serve the LORD with gladness: come before his presence
with singing. Know ye that the LORD he is God: it is
he that hath made us, and not we ourselves; we are his
people and the sheep of his pasture. Enter into his gates
with thanksgiving, and into his courts with praise;
be thankful unto him and bless his name. For the
LORD is good; his mercy is everlasting;
and his truth endureth to all generations.*
Psalm 100 KJV

*B*ecause we have been saved by God's only Son, we must never lose hope in the priceless gifts of eternal love and eternal life. And, because we are so richly blessed, we must approach our Heavenly Father with reverence and thanksgiving.

Sometimes, in our rush "to get things done," we simply don't stop long enough to pause and thank our Creator for the countless blessings He has bestowed upon us. But when we slow down and express our gratitude to the One who made us, we enrich our own lives and the lives of those around us.

Thanksgiving should become a habit, a regular part of our daily routines. God has blessed us beyond measure, and we owe Him everything, including our eternal praise. Let us praise Him today, tomorrow, and throughout eternity.

Give thanks in all circumstances; for this is God's will for you in Christ Jesus.

1 Thessalonians 5:18 NIV

Telling the Lord how much you love
Him and why is what praise and
worship are all about.
Lisa Whelchel

Praise the LORD! Oh give thanks to
the LORD, for He is good;
For His lovingkindness is everlasting.
Psalm 106:1 NASB

The act of thanksgiving is a demonstration
of the fact that you are going to
trust and believe God.
Kay Arthur

Thanks be to God for
his indescribable gift!
2 Corinthians 9:15 NIV

God is worthy of our praise and
is pleased when we come before Him
with thanksgiving.
Shirley Dobson

Preoccupy my thoughts with
Your praise, beginning today.

Joni Eareckson Tada

It is only with gratitude that life
becomes rich.
Dietrich Bonhoeffer

As you therefore have received Christ
Jesus the Lord, so walk in Him, having
been firmly rooted and now being built up
in Him and established in your faith, just
as you were instructed, and overflowing
with gratitude.
Colossians 2:6-7 NASB

Rejoice always; pray without ceasing.
1 Thessalonians 5:16–17 NASB

Praise Him! Praise Him!
Tell of His excellent greatness.
Praise Him! Praise Him!
Ever in joyful song!

Fanny Crosby

This is my story, this is my song,
praising my Savior,
all the day long.

Fanny Crosby

A Prayer from the Garden

Lord, I offer thanksgiving and praise to You. Let me share the joyous news of Jesus Christ with a world that needs His transformation and His salvation. Today, let me express my thanksgiving, Father, not just through my words but also through my deeds . . . and may all the glory be Yours.

Amen